HOARDERS

HOARDERS

KATE DURBIN

WAVE BOOKS   SEATTLE & NEW YORK

Published by Wave Books

www.wavepoetry.com

Copyright © 2021 by Kate Durbin

Wave Books titles are distributed to the trade by

Consortium Book Sales and Distribution

Phone: 800-283-3572 / SAN 631-760X

Library of Congress Cataloging-in-Publication Data

Names: Durbin, Kate, author.

Title: Hoarders / Kate Durbin.

Description: First Edition. | Seattle : Wave Books, [2021]

Identifiers: LCCN 2020038255

ISBN 9781950268146 (hardcover)

ISBN 9781950268139 (paperback)

Subjects: LCGFT: Poetry.

Classification: LCC PS3604.U7277 H63 2021 | DDC 811/.6—dc23

LC record available at https://lccn.loc.gov/2020038255

Designed by Crisis

Printed in the United States of America

9 8 7 6 5 4 3 2 1

First Edition

Wave Books 092

MARLENA

TOPANGA CANYON, CALIFORNIA

I'm Marlena, the worst hoarder on planet Pink Sands Yankee Candle

My house is like a bomb went off at Walmart shattered seashell wreaths, rainbow dream catchers tangled with LED hummingbird wind chimes, tie-dyed lion tapestry with a hole in the lion's face, Drew Barrymore Flower Home Collection plates with half-eaten Luna bars and dead wasps

I was a fashion model for many years in Europe moth-eaten Balenciaga dresses

Then my husband and I fell in love photo of young Marlena and a man hugging in front of a private jet, her hair in pigtails, her midriff tanned and toned

Our relationship was storybook ceramic plate of two chickens pecking, smeared with crystallized honey

After a few weeks he proposed sunbleached hippie boho fabric lovebirds

I felt like we stepped onto a magic carpet and just flew Cost Plus World Market mandala pillows, Indian elephant throw, crushed banana chips, blackened bananas, crumpled Sunset magazine pages, stuffed panda in lotus pose on Marlena's bed

But after our daughter was born, my husband started dating other women secretly dozens of Louis Vuitton bags under the bed

When I found out, I just wanted a divorce on the front door: KEEP OUT ABSOLUTELY NO SOLICITORS—THIS MEANS YOU, BEWARE OF DOG sign, card that says OUR LADY OF LOURDES PRAY FOR US and underneath, in shaky handwriting, HELP ME GOD

I felt suicidal, but I had my two-year-old daughter to think of photo of Marlena's daughter in pigtails and big Chanel sunglasses playing the piano

That was a very hard time for me, completely lost in the bathroom, dusty makeup brushes, goopy concealer, murky bottles of Dior nail polish, melted Cherries on Snow Yankee Candle with grey hairs stuck in the wax

I started collecting Whole Foods 365 products

My kitchen sink is totally full Organic Turkish Apricots, Cheddar Bunnies, Sea Salt Avocado Oil Canyon Cut Potato Chips, Himalayan Pink Salt Popcorn, Cookie Dough Collagen Protein Bars, Organic Goji Berries, Blue Magic Cashew Milk, Majestic Sprouted Hummus

My hoarding has caused a terrible rift between me and my American Girl doll with a destroyed face

She started taking my things and throwing them out without asking, so I put all of her old things in plastic bags Little Mermaid Ariel doll smeared with marker, Easy Bake Oven filled with old crumbs, Lil Miss Makeup doll with red cheeks and lips and chewed fingers, clump of My Little Ponies

I said she wasn't welcome at the house anymore dirty lips pillow that says KISS ME

I want desperately to change Marlena digging in neighborhood trash bins, a flashlight strapped to her head; she pulls out Chase credit card statements, Styrofoam food containers, Starbucks reusable plastic cups

But I don't like when people throw out things that still work Marlena testing a Sharpie on an electricity bill

When they put trash in the recycling bin, I move it to the trash Marlena carefully moving a Chiquita banana peel from the recycling to the trash

When plants in the neighborhood are not properly watered, I do Marlena facing a tree, pouring water on its roots; her slender legs and her thin neck, her grey hair

Even though this is trash to most humans on the planet, it isn't trash to me Marlena slowly reaching into a giant pile of unopened Whole Foods items on her kitchen floor and lifting out a bottle of water; Marlena somehow pulling a clean cup from the eruption inside the sink; Marlena pouring herself a cup of water to drink

CHUCK

BISBEE, ARIZONA

I'm Chuck, and I'm paintbrush with natural hair

I love to paint most anything, but my favorite subject is the female figure painting of a naked blonde in a kitchen chair staring at a wall

They're vulnerable, and at their most feminine, when you see the whole body, your model is the inspiration for the painting, and the subject of the painting, all wrapped up in one painting of two nearly naked women wearing southwestern style shawls that expose their breasts, one reclining on the couch, the other on the floor next to a bull skull, hand over crotch

I have hundreds of paintings of sketches of naked women with coffee stains

When you walk into the studio now, I don't have much open space painting of a naked blonde crossing her legs

I started filling it up with oil paints and measuring tape

It's perverse because it defeats my original purpose in buying that big painting of a red building

Painting is the primary motivating force in my life, and I've lost the space to painting of a naked blonde with red lipstick

A lot of artists start collecting little things as inspiration painting of a naked blonde eating an orange

Nature abhors a vacuum and I guess I abhor empty spaces painting of the desert outside his house

I would not want to live if I couldn't paint crucifix

I used to be married, and clutter wasn't a problem still life of grapes spilling out of a bowl

My first marriage was the happiest I've ever been painting of a naked blonde on a couch with a pillow under her butt

But then my wife had surgery after giving birth to my kids naked blonde lying on a drop cloth with her hands over her breasts

I couldn't handle seeing her in pain half-painted painting of a naked blonde with her eyes shut

She sought attention from someone else PEZ dispenser of Paul Revere

I would have upsurges of anger every day, you know, at blank canvases

I got into alcohol pretty seriously empty sketchbooks

I started collecting guns painting of a naked blonde hunched over, clutching her stomach

I was angry at my wife, because she wanted to have affairs and I couldn't take that painting of a naked blonde on top of a German Tanks & Fighting Vehicles of World War II book

So it was either move out or do something violent with her painting of a naked blonde with a boot print on it

This is my favorite painting of a naked blonde sitting on a couch next to a half man, half javelina

I used this beautiful model, I used her several times actually, and I have many painting of a naked blonde with closed eyes next to a potted plant; behind the plant crouches a javelina man

I wanted it to be like Beauty and the Beast and he's trying to engage her in conversation or explain himself to her and she's just blissfully unaware palette knife

I always felt that I was doing a self-portrait when I was doing the beast, the javelina painting of a naked blonde asleep in bed next to a javelina man

It's like my alter ego painting of the javelina man and a naked blonde in the expressionist style

Any time you get a javelina and a pretty lady, you're gonna have some conflict painting of a naked blonde running through the desert chased by a javelina man

Well, I've married some beautiful sketch of a naked woman prostrate

None of them lasted painting of a naked blonde with angel wings knifing the heart of a javelina man

You can't just give away beautiful things naked woman lying on the ground, eyes shut, tongue hanging out

Painting is the bedrock, like the Grand Canyon—hard and it sustains

LINDA

WASHINGTON, DC

My name is Linda, and I love cooking rotting food

My kitchen has all kinds of wonderful molds, a Mongolian fire-pot, got that bag of sugar with mice in it

Food is like creativity and possibilities in life jar of old nuts with bugs

But I don't have a working refrigerator black sludge

When I buy food, I hang it from the chandelier in order to keep the rats from getting into Safeway bag slowly rotating with moldy hummus, CVS bag with expired Special K, Yes! Organic Market bag with blackened corn, Safeway bag with shriveled lettuce, CVS bag with expired Froot Loops, Yes! Organic Market bag with puckered granny apples, Safeway bag with sprouting onions, CVS bag with expired Cheerios, Yes! Organic Market bag with old organic indecipherable

It's as if somebody took a municipal garbage dump and just dumped it into kitchen cabinets streaked with brown goo

Or a swamp thing growing a new life form in the basement tub
of old chicken bones, sweating

Or an evil witch from a fairy tale rotting peach

Or Texas Chainsaw Massacre dead squirrel in a butter dish

My daughter threatens me that everything could be condemned,
that the house could fall in upside down egg carton with a post-
card of the sky on it

Because I'm not doing enough to maintain kitchen sink piled with years old dirty dishes

This is a million dollar neighborhood and the neighbors are not happy, so they've called the zoning board smashed Starbucks cup with X2 2M N ~~WE~~ M handwritten and rat poop on it

I've been living in this house thirty years, but it was much different before 25-year-old blackened candy

It was spotless on the kitchen mantel, a figurine of an Italian villa wrapped in plastic

My husband was an abusive sociopath fossilized rat

It was like living with Jim Jones dirty unmarked bottles of black liquids

It was constantly up and down—very good and very bad 20-year-old hot sauce that belonged to her husband that she doesn't even like

I love you, I love you, I love you, move out, I can't stand you rotting apple, apple, apple; something in the peanut butter jar that isn't peanut butter

Even though I kept a beautiful home, he convinced me I was mag-got larva

He didn't like me to do any artwork or any crafts, so that's why I channeled my creativity toward The Taste of Mexico, The Jewish Cook Book, Flavors of Portugal, From Hearth to Cookstove, Vegetarian Times, Scandinavian Cooking, First Ladies Cook Book, Julia Child's Kitchen Wisdom

My daughter tried to convince me the food I cooked was weird apple pie with raw chicken hearts

What's weird about dried mealworm bodies ground up to make nice cookies oven window black with mold

She encouraged me to give up cooking and do more painting Linda made of herself looking into a hand mirror with harrowed eyes; surrounding the mirror in the painting are perfume bottles and flowers

I save old soda cans and turn the tin snips into flowers dried orange peels Linda put on the radiator so when it turns on the house smells of oranges and rot

My husband kept me from going to the doctor because I would have found out he'd given me venereal disease, so it got worse and worse flies buzzing room to room

He left me when I was sick and then I started to lose my grip on the house over the kitchen window, a cloth with cut fruit on it

I had gone through so much, I had cried so much, I'd gone into a frozen state old ice chest piled with oozing Breyers ice cream, popsicle sticks smothered in goo, dirty ceramic snowman, First Alert smoke alarm box, burlap Jesus, Marcus Aurelius bust wearing sunglasses

One day I might make a final mistake and eat cracked pineapple jar with something black inside

SHELLEY

WARREN, MICHIGAN

I'm Shelley, I'm 59, and I'm a retired salesclerk Tim Gunn Collection Barbie wearing a pencil skirt; on the box is a picture of Tim Gunn in a suit and glasses next to the words QUALITY TASTE STYLE

I guess I have to admit I am a hoarder thousands of Barbies

I love to play Barbies inside boxes labeled with their years of creation: 1959, 1967, 1977, 1986, etc.

They have all different character Barbies I Love Lucy Barbie, Scarlett O'Hara Barbie, Swan Lake Ballerina Barbie, Haunted Beauty Ghost Barbie, Firefighter Barbie, Sugar Plum Fairy Barbie, Hera Barbie, Mary Poppins Barbie, Architect Barbie, Faith Hill Barbie, Presidential Candidate Barbie, Kate Winslet in Titanic Barbie, Harpist Angel Barbie, Army Medic Barbie, Quinceañera Barbie, Hard Rock Cafe Barbie, Splash 'n Color Change Hair Barbie, Stars 'n Stripes Barbie, Film Director Barbie, Princess of the Danish Court Barbie, I Dream of Jeannie Barbie, Marie Antoinette Barbie, Tippi Hedren in The Birds Barbie, Grandma Barbie, Full House Barbie, Game Developer Barbie, Juicy Couture Beverly Hills Barbie, Gymnast Barbie, Claude Monet Water Lily Barbie, Dentist Barbie, Wizard of Oz Dorothy Barbie, Barbie Loves Elvis Barbie, Marine Corps Barbie, Elizabeth Taylor in Cleopatra Barbie, Pioneer Barbie, Victorian Elegance Barbie, Chinese Empress Barbie, Newborn Baby Doctor Barbie, Summer Splendor Barbie, Jewel Secrets Barbie, Gustav Klimt Barbie, Diva Barbie, Race Car Driver Barbie, Twilight Saga Bella Barbie, Police Officer Barbie, Aphrodite Barbie, Computer Engineer Barbie, Rock Star Barbie, Pierrot Barbie, Olympic Skater Barbie, NASCAR Barbie, Astronaut Barbie, Haunted Beauty Zombie Bride Barbie, Ancient Rome Gladiator Barbie, Andy Warhol Barbie, etc.

I know pretty much what I have, but it's just gotten out of hand
original teenage fashion model Barbie from 1959 with winged
eyeliner next to Walk & Potty Pup Barbie with pink leash and
tiny nuggets of poo

I have the outfits, shoes, matching Tupperware stacked to the
ceiling filled with Barbie accessories

The basement is totally covered with dolls from the movie In-
surgent

In the kids' rooms, I have a lot of storage of my dolls too two Bratz dolls huddled on a tiny bed; the pink haired one is holding herself as if she is cold; the other has green skin, a tattered shirt, and a leg brace; next to the Bratz is a their-size Christmas tree

I spent most of my paychecks on tiny Barbie ornaments

Things have just piled up shelf with Scooby Doo, Curious George, Frankenstein's monster, frowning Statue of Liberty pillow, headless Marilyn Monroe Barbie in a silver gown

Almost every room is touched with the mess I Love Jesus heart night light shining on Elvis Ken in sparkling jumpsuit on a bathroom counter crammed with Avon products

My hoarding has left my family in debt and my house in disrepair shelf of Barbies with disheveled hair

Last couple of years we've had a problem with the Barbie Dream House with a pink plastic roof

We had a leak, so I hung a tarp from the ceiling to drain the water into Jacuzzi Barbie in a Barbie Jacuzzi

I never want anyone to see the second Barbie Dream House stuffed with monkeys wearing Planet Hollywood shirts

Because of all the mess in the house, we couldn't have someone come in to check out Barbie arm sticking out of a Target bag

Because I'm embarrassed David Bowie poster overlooking a massive pile of Barbies with a Hunger Games Katniss Everdeen Barbie on top

My mother lives with us and she can't even walk down the hallway because there's so much tiny Barbie shoes

All that's open is a chair, a TV, a path to the bathroom, a path to grandmother asleep on a recliner in the living room, a Christmas Cookie Yankee Candle flickering next to her; behind her, a pile of Barbies with a skeleton mask on top; in the corner, a Cabbage Patch doll in pioneer clothes reclines at the same angle as her; a glittering snowman watches

My mother sleeps in the chair because her bedroom is so full of
In Touch magazines including one with Michael Jackson wearing a dust mask on the cover

My daughter came in and said if you don't fix this I'm going to call the authorities, put Grandma in pink Barbie lunch pail

And now my husband's alcoholism is triggered by Barbie driving a pink Corvette, alone

I was getting mad at him, so tit for tat, I would buy a doll, and he would go on a drinking binge Viva Pink Avon nail polish next to pregnant Barbie with magnetic removable belly

That was really when I started the snowball effect of all this collecting hundreds of Beanie Babies watching as she shops on eBay; Beanie Baby reindeer, Beanie Baby bat, Beanie Baby panda, Beanie Baby lemur, Beanie Baby snow leopard, Beanie Baby harp seal, Princess Diana Beanie Baby bear; inside the Beanie Babies, legs of smothered Barbies jut out into the air

I'm scared clown from It doll, grinning

Why ruin everyone's life for dolls? Frights, Camera, Action!
doll with blue skin wearing a tattered dress

CRAIG

GREENVILLE, SOUTH CAROLINA

I'm Craig, I'm 58 years old, and I'm tattered American flag next to a boot

I spent most of my life collecting rare and pretty things THIS CLUTTER IS MY BREAD AND BUTTER framed calligraphy

Even I admit it's way too crowded crooked paths between stacks of boxes, thrift store paintings, mildewed newspapers, Southern knickknacks and antiques

I dated my ex for five years bust of a bonneted pioneer woman propping up a Southern Comfort box

During that time she complained because I would go weeks without a bath, weeks without changing my shirt or pants salt and pepper shakers of a boy and girl in antebellum clothes dancing, covered in black dust

My landlord just learned from the codes inspector that I've been living here without electricity and water Craig sweating on the front stoop, petting a pit bull

If I don't get my house cleaned up in just a couple of days I'm gonna be evicted, I'm gonna lose my dog, I'm gonna lose stacks of rotting Encyclopaedia Britannicas

I'm diabetic and my medicine is not refrigerated now—I depend on that insulin needle resting in a Southern Deposit Bank ashtray

I can't live under these conditions Craig lifting up his dirty t-shirt and sticking a needle in his belly

My daddy was a soldier in World War II and served in the elite SS troops black and white photo of a young, smiling man in a Nazi uniform

He was from a long line of butchers, a long line of soldiers, a long line of white Jesus in five foot oak frame

All my daddy ever wanted was a boy baby doll face ripped from the body and no eyes

But he was tough to grow up under, and he rode me unmercifully because he wanted me to be way more than I ever could boar's head on the wall with glass eyes and sharp teeth

I told him, Daddy, I'm not gonna do anything like that Deutschland Erwacht belt clip with a swastika on it

Even he had to concede I'm not the guy for the job LORD, HELP ME TO DO WHAT I CAN, WHERE I AM, WITH WHAT I HAVE wall sign

I tried to be tough like my daddy but I just never measured up to his traditional German beer stein with a relief of the Black Forest on it

He wanted me to be a leader in the Germanic cause, a leader of the Fourth Reich photo of tiny Craig in lederhosen

My daddy was the cook of the house wood carving of a skeleton tucked between knives and forks

At dinner one day he asked me how I liked his food and I said, it was good Dad, and he goes, I'm glad you liked it because that was your pet rabbit wind blowing through a hole in the ceiling

That was the first time I started to look at him as a frightening, murdering, bad guy white Jesus wood plaque next to a faux tribal devil mask from Hobby Lobby

I don't need lights in my house, I know every inch candlelight flickering on a garden gnome's face

I am careful with crumbs dirt falling through the hole in the ceiling

I have fought rats and I have fought mice antique German hunting knife made of stag bone

I put so much poison in this house that big red gobs rose up everywhere on me abstract painting with violent red strokes

Do you see that painting hanging up on the wall past the edge of the boxes, I expect that might be a $100,000 painting based on photo of an iceberg, the best-selling stock photo of all time

Everything I got means something to me, everything I got has some sort of value to it, so when you pick things up, pick them up tenderly woman's ceramic hands sprouting from a cornucopia, grasping

I know you have to hurry, but if you can do this out of kindness to marble pelvis of David in the back of a 1-800-GOT-JUNK? truck

CATHY

CENTRALIA, ILLINOIS

I'm Cathy, I'm a medical lab technician rhinestone tiara

I have five kids—four boys and crystal serving platter

I've worked night shift for like twenty-one years and I haven't been able to keep a house sewing machine still inside the box

Most days I don't see the sun sequin lashes sleeping mask from Claire's Accessories

I collect lots of things but especially clothes Windsor Wildfire prom dress, $14.99 marked down from $149.50, Talbot's Striped Flounce dress, $129.00 marked down from $169.00, Charlotte Russe lace and chiffon bridesmaid dress, $39.99 marked down from $49.99

My life is kind of dedicated to shopping David's Bridal halter wedding gown with a blusher veil

It's like an adventure maze of Target Lakeside Collection pastel decorative pumpkins that spell out THANKS

I like the color and I like the bling pink rhinestone cupcake clutch

I am constantly ordering off TV sitNcycle

Every single day it's almost like there's another package at the front door package ripped open with LuLaRoe winking Minnie Mouse leggings, LuLaRoe thorny rose leggings, LuLaRoe fire truck hydrant ax boot alarm leggings

I like the satisfaction of having something new JTV heart-shaped pink topaz ring in a box that says GIFT TO MYSELF

I've wasted a lot of money three identical Forever 21 beaded chiffon maxi dresses

$50,000 or more in credit card debt David's Bridal strapless corset wedding gown with a chapel veil

I have a sickness pink medicine ball

For security reasons, I want to stay married stair stepper

Do we really love each other? Probably not Fairytale Bride Barbie and Fairytale Groom Ken in separate boxes on a Live Laugh Love shelf from Target

I don't want my children to have a broken home Thomas Kinkade for Target puzzle of a painting of a snowy cottage, windows aglow with golden light

But technically it's a broken home already paper plate that says DO NOT FLUSH THE TOILET in Sharpie

There might be something in here that might still be important to me Lexmark printer still in the box

I'm not sure what it is second Lexmark printer still in the box

My family thinks I'm selfish five Swarovski crystal encrusted Starbucks cups

You know what, I don't believe that Keurig coffee pod carousel with Hyper-Caffeinated Vanilla Blast, Chocolate Glazed Donut, Crème Brûlée, Cinnamon Roll, Macadamia Nut Cookie, Bananas Foster Flambé, Italian Chocolate Cheesecake, Peanut Butter & Jelly Sandwich, Cake Boss Bada Boom, Mudslide, Death by Coffee, Death Wish pods

I really didn't ever like boys Wayne Gretzky bobbleheads buried to their necks in lavender bath beads from Bed Bath & Beyond

I really didn't want another faded Space Jam bedsheet under a pile of brand new Wayfair butterfly pillowcases

And why throw away like a brand new old Pinkalicious Maybelline nail polish

*Even though this has dust on it, I would like to shake this out and
use* David's Bridal mermaid illusion wedding dress with a cathedral veil

I'm chronically disappointed plastic snowshoe that says I BELIEVE in glitter cursive

I've never even liked Christmas filthy Olaf the snowman oven mitt

I am like literally telling the truth

NOAH & ALLIE

CHICAGO, ILLINOIS

Allie: *I'm an avid reader and aspiring writer who collects a lot of* books filling the house so there are only narrow crevices to worm through; windows black with paperbacks so no natural light comes in; floors buckling under the weight of overstuffed bookshelves

My husband Noah and I have been married for forty-two wonderful, crowded years Noah's plaid tie tucked in The Canterbury Tales for a bookmark; Allie's plaid shirt stuffed on a shelf between Nancy Drew's Clue in the Diary and Hardy Boys' Disappearing Floor

Noah: *I'm a teacher and a book lover from way back* Mystics and Messiahs, Basic Teachings of the Great Philosophers, Paganism Book

Allie: *In this house, we have two very familiar phrases—"I love you" and "timberrrrr!"* books behind the front door, collapsing

We have books nine feet high in some places Hurricanes and Tornadoes, Jack and the Beanstalk, The Castle, The Wall

On the first floor it is wall-to-wall books, with only a narrow path through Versailles, Great Houses of Washington, DC

Noah: *Getting up and down the stairs can be a challenge* Gaudi, Allergy, William Morris, Corpse, William Morris, Allergy, Gaudi

Allie: *Books are our passion, we are omnivores of every kind of information* Exam Cram MCSE Core, MCSE Network Plus, Installing Debian GNU/Linux, Windows 98, Practical Windows, Presenting Java, Official BONG, Access 2000

Noah: *You can find a book about anything* Crocheting for Dummies, Screenwriting for Dummies, Organic Chemistry for Dummies, British Sign Language for Dummies, The Ancient Egyptians for Dummies, The British Monarchy for Dummies, Catholic High School Entrance Exams for Dummies, Composting for Dummies, Atheism for Dummies, Ballet for Dummies, Baby Massage for Dummies, Dad's Guide to Baby's First Year for Dummies, Bird Watching for Dummies, Dog Photography for Dummies, Second Life for Dummies, Solving Cryptic Crosswords for Dummies, Workplace Conflict Resolution Essentials for Dummies New Zealand and Australian Edition, Work/Life Balance for Dummies, Veterans Benefits for Dummies, Starting an iPhone Application Business for Dummies, Acid Reflux Diet for Dummies, Cooking with Chia for Dummies, Building Chicken Coops for Dummies, Wilderness Survival for Dummies, Being a Great Dad for Dummies, Body Language for Dummies, Boosting Self-Esteem for Dummies, Build a Better Life Box Set for Dummies

Allie: *Noah and I met in college and we were birds of a feather* Sisson's Synonyms

Noah: *There was a happy collision of mutual interests* Scottish Architecture, Cop Speak, Gun Dog Breeds, Alternative Medications, Embracing the Moon

Allie: *Noah and I knew each other eighteen days before we got married* Turning Life into Fiction, Romeo and Juliet

Noah: *A few weeks after getting married, they had a book sale at the university and I came home with two shopping bags of books and my bride's eyes got big* The Dollar Crisis, The Great Gatsby

Allie: *Unfortunately, my kitchen is not a kitchen anymore* Cooking Without a Kitchen

Noah: *It takes a little bit of dexterity to get to the stove* Gumby Goes to the Sun

Allie: *So mainly we eat* dusty Jell-O boxes and Mike's Hard Cranberry Lemonade balanced on Little Golden Books on the stove top; inside the stove, The Joy of Cooking and other remaindered cookbooks; fridge doors ajar, shelves filled with Harlequins

Allie: *Next to my bed, I have a pile of books; in the middle of the night sometimes, it all comes crashing down on me* Shakespeare's Tragedies, Greek Classics, The Civil War, Gone with the Wind, Pearl Harbor, PERL, 1812: The War That Forged a Nation, Return of Depression Economics and the Crisis of 2008, The Battle of Britain, The Battle Plan for Prayer, Terrorism, Counter-Terrorism, Great Gambles, World History, German Verbs, Introduction to Statistics, Wicca for Beginners, Wicca for Men

Noah: *I think the conclusion we reached is* uneven bookshelf with a paperback of Hermann Hesse's Siddhartha precariously propping it up

Noah: *Uh, we have reached the limit* another bookshelf toppling, books falling

Allie: *My biggest fear is my husband's* Hurst's The Heart 10th Edition

He has a condition and anything can happen at any time and the EMTs absolutely could not get him out of the Canadian Rockies Access Guide

The city patrol to make sure everybody has a parking pass, and they inferred from the stuff in our car that the house looked like UFO CRASH, Tom Cruise Answer Book, Gray's Anatomy, BIG BOOK OF PIZZA

Noah: *They left a note on the door with intent to inspect the premises* The Real Men in Black: Evidence, Famous Cases, and True Stories of These Mysterious Men and Their Connection to the UFO Phenomena

Allie: *I don't want to think about what would happen if the city came into* The Illuminati: Secret Society That Hijacked the World

Allie: *When we moved into this house in 1977, we took out some of the appliances and just started moving books in* bookcases where a washer and dryer would go; books on the toilet and books in the sink; books on the floor so when they walk their feet slide around

Noah: *We moved in perhaps with 30,000 books; now it could be 500,000* Unsolved Disappearances in the Great Smoky Mountains

Allie: *We are soul mates; we don't have to be physical on a bed together to connect* two single mattresses in separate rooms, each surrounded by walls of books

Noah: *I don't see how books can be a danger to anybody* Berlin Wall, Bush Agenda, Gettysburg Jury, Elections, America Eats!

Books don't bite The Science of Jurassic Park and The Lost World, Dracula

JIM

ORLAND, CALIFORNIA

I'm Jim, I'm a retired policeman garden windmill

Some old men go to casinos and some go fishing rusty Folgers coffee cans

My enjoyment is waking up and going to yard sales and swap meets Yukon Deluxe gold prospecting kit

I see this thing or that thing and it don't need to be going to the dump rusty wagon wheel

So I bring it home and tinker with tilted mailbox with bird feathers in it

That's why I got stuff like this blown out tire

You just gotta know what to do with wet book of matches

There's hammers, there's axles, there's rusted clawfoot bathtub

If I see a beautiful tool, I'll pick it up and bring it home busted bench vise

Since 2007, the city has been pressing me to clean up toilet with no seat

I live in America dirty football helmet

You own property and pay the taxes over broken box springs

People, they have the right to live on their property as they please men's Hanes underwear with skid marks

To me, it's not a cracked birdbath

There's metal, there's bikes, there's sewing machines and other machinery that I will rebuild Bendix washing machine from 1947 with a house finch nesting inside

I thought maybe I'd have a little resale shop or thrift store or something like that red wheelbarrow with no wheels

But it never seemed to work right smashed Arm & Hammer laundry detergent bottle

I never got along too well with people shattered rearview mirror

This is how I deal crushed Red Bulls

This stuff gives me something to work with, to piddle with and clean out rusty waterspout

I was a boxer and in the Marine Corps Jim's yard filled with ancient stoves, refrigerators and sinks, bent bike wheels, used up cans of Barbasol and Old Spice, tin pots, rusty cast iron frying pan, Vietnam War helmet with 1968 and 1969 and the months of the year written on it in black Sharpie, each month carefully crossed out; bullet shells and casings for land mines scattered in the dirt; in the distance, Jim's house, its front door shut, curtains blocking the windows; the shadow of many large unknown things press against the curtains; in front of the house sits Jim in a motorized wheelchair, a tiny American flag stuck in the back

Now I'm an old man ten-gallon hat

Give me a little hope Everlast punching bag with duct tape hold-
ing it together

I'm gonna get my health back and punch that bag

ALICE

BELOIT, WISCONSIN

I'm Alice, and I'm a cashier cat inside a hole in the wall, yellow eyes peering

Come on little girl, you want to go inside? house with a satellite dish and dark windows, surrounded by woods

I'm not into jewels and shoes nine paper plates with wet cat food, Alice's Birkenstocks lying near

I'd give the shirt off my cat hair lining the walls, floor, and furniture in a downy coat

I like cats because I feel they're entertaining bathroom sink filled with empty water jugs; a black cat tucked between jugs, asleep

I always thought, the more the merrier white cat dragging through the hall, seven kittens at her teats

The reason I collect cats is I have this feeling in me that I'm helping save something exercise bike with rusted wheels, surrounded by shit

They're farm cats, they're not litter box trained so they go all over the floor—you can't reach one side of the kitchen because there's a huge pile of shit, a mottled brown kitten on weak legs trying to climb out of the shit

I let them in and feed them and they just stay grey cat with a gash in its shoulder eating from a china plate

I was spaying every stray that comes around kitten suckling its mother on a dirty cheetah print blanket

Then the money ran out red bedsheets in the windows, sun leaking through

After that you know what happens cats on the stairs like streaks of light

They breed and they breed cats on banisters coated in hair and dust

If they took away all my cats it would kill me two kittens facing each other on a soiled mattress; one has a gap where its eye should be

My son has threatened to call the sheriff's office to do a welfare check grey cat hiding behind a bedsheet

I think I just am too emotional and I don't want anything to die dead cat slumped against a wall

I've had quite a few losses destroyed mostly empty room with a china cabinet in the far corner and unbroken china inside

My father died of a heart attack right in front of me floor torn up so only the plywood is left

I didn't know what to do at that age, I didn't know how to call cat on the kitchen countertop, eyes oozing

I felt I was the one that caused cat squatting and shitting on the countertop

So I think later on in my years having this many cats was a need for me empty cat food bowl on the bed where a pillow would go

I'm just so afraid of death, you know, I just try and keep things alive Alice lying in her bed surrounded by file folders, clutching a kitten to her cheek

When my first cat got killed, I put him in the freezer because I wanted to get him cremated among Ziploc bags, a tiny black cat, body frosted, ears missing

I probably have in frozen and refrigerated cats between 75–100 if not more orange juice, soy sauce, and milk next to the refrigerated cats

Now I know I should be disposing of them but I just love my little cats and I don't want them to leave several cats frozen together in a tangle of feet and fur

I just feel awful, I'm a failure and that's how my whole life has been one fresh shit among old shits

My cats probably have worms, they probably have ear mites, there's probably feline leukemia, feline AIDS running through black kitten whose hind legs won't work lurching across the floor

I had a kitten and there was so much ammonia in the air that its eyeballs popped out grey cat with its eyes crusted shut

I don't even know how this started hiking boots under the bed, soles thick with shit

I can't even say anymore that I love animals because I've treated them so horrible Alice stirring wet food on a paper plate with her finger then feeding it to one of the tiniest kittens by prying its mouth open and gently placing the food on its small, pink tongue

DOROTHY

TOWANDA, KANSAS

I'm Dorothy, a home health care worker VHS tape

I've been watching every day since I was a kid bookcase filled
with Sesame Street (1969–present)

I've been recording for years, and as technology has progressed,
so has my shelves of data; strata of Betamax covered with dust
and lint under shelves bowing with stacks of VHS with faded
handwritten labels below shelves of DVDs in cracked cases; on
top of the bookcase, spindles of new, unused DVDs

The living room is Dorothy eating popcorn out of a Thomas Kinkade snowy windmill popcorn tin, watching The Bachelorette on a flatscreen; in the show, the bachelorette is holding a rose and crying

The bedroom is Dorothy in a double bed, an I Love Lucy blanket with jam stains pulled over her; across the room, a TV plays 60 Minutes; in the show, set against a red background, a stopwatch is ticking

The laundry room is Dorothy hanging faded Mickey Mouse print scrubs on a clothesline; a TV on a broken dryer plays Hoarders; in the show a woman is crying, surrounded by dead cats

The bathroom is Dorothy washing her hair in the sink, head tilted to watch CSI on a countertop TV; water droplets bead on the screen, distorting things; in the show, detectives look at a woman's corpse; behind Dorothy in the bathroom, a bathtub filled with a sea of black tapes

The kitchen is Dorothy washing a faded Tweety Bird mug; a small TV on a crumb-filled windowsill playing Little House on the Prairie; in the show, two girls in bonnets look out the back of a covered wagon as it jostles slowly through a field

The backyard is tubs filled with ruined tapes and rainwater

My kids say I ought to do something else with my time, but I can do what I want with bookcase of VHS and DVDs all labeled Today Show (1952–present)

I guess I'm afraid of not seeing The Walking Dead (2010–present), Downton Abbey (2010–2015), Chopped (2007–present), Breaking Bad (2008–2013), Mad Men (2007–2015), The Big Bang Theory (2007–2019), Keeping Up with the Kardashians (2006–present), Grey's Anatomy (2005–present), Intervention (2005–present), Hell's Kitchen (2005–present), How I Met Your Mother (2005–2014), The Office (2005–2013), Lost (2004–2010), Project Runway (2004–present), Queer Eye for the Straight Guy (2003–2007) Ellen DeGeneres (2003–present), American Idol (2002–present), The Amazing Race (2001–present), Gilmore Girls (2000–2007), Survivor (2000–present), Big Brother (2000–present), Law & Order: Special Victims Unit (1999–present), Judge Joe Brown (1997–2013), Sex and the City (1998–2004), That '70s Show (1998–2006), Charmed (1998–2006), The Daily Show (1996–present), Judge Judy (1996–present), Rosie O'Donnell (1996–2002), Xena: Warrior Princess (1995–2001), Road Rules (1995–2007), Party of Five (1994–2000), ER (1994–2009), Friends (1994–2004), Ricki Lake (1992–2004), Melrose Place (1992–1999), Dr. Quinn, Medicine Woman (1993–1998), Barney and Friends (1992–2009), Ghostwriter (1992–1995), Hangin' with Mr. Cooper (1992–1997), Rugrats (1990–2006), Home Improvement (1991–1999), Dinosaurs (1991–1994), Jerry Springer (1991–2018), Maury Povich (1991–present), The Montel Williams Show (1991–2008), Jenny Jones (1991–2003), The Simpsons (1989–present), Murphy Brown (1988–1998), Unsolved Mysteries (1987–2010), Star Trek: The Next Generation (1987–1994), DuckTales (1987–1990), Geraldo (1987–1998), Oprah (1986–2011), L.A. Law (1986–1994), Pee-wee's Playhouse (1986–1991), Growing Pains (1985–1992), The Golden Girls (1985–1992), MacGyver (1985–1992), The Care Bears (1985–1988), The Cosby Show (1984–1992), Night Court (1984–92), Heathcliff (1980–1984), Sally Jessy Raphael (1983–2002), Knight Rider (1982–1986), Cheers (1982–1993), Family Ties (1982–1989), Dynasty (1981–1989), The People's Court (1981–1993), The Dukes of Hazzard (1979–1985), Dallas (1978–1991), 20/20 (1978–present), Three's Company (1976–1984), CHiPs (1977–1983), The Love Boat (1977–1987), Charlie's Angels (1976–1981), Welcome Back, Kotter (1975–1979), Happy Days (1974–1984), The Young and the Restless (1973–present), The Waltons (1972–1981), Sanford and Son (1972–1977), All in the Family (1971–1979), Monday Night Football (1970–present), The Mary Tyler Moore Show (1970–1977), The Days of Our Lives (1965–present), General Hospital (1963–present), Mister Rogers' Neighborhood (1968–2001), As the World Turns (1956–2010), Guiding Light (1952–2009)

I couldn't possibly watch them all if I sat down today and started

HANNAH

BOTHELL, WASHINGTON

My name is Hannah and I AM ME poster on wall with a rose in the center that says IN ALL THE WORLD, THERE IS NO ONE ELSE EXACTLY LIKE ME. EVERYTHING THAT COMES OUT OF ME IS AUTHENTICALLY ME. BECAUSE I ALONE CHOSE IT—I OWN EVERYTHING ABOUT ME. MY BODY, MY FEELINGS, MY MOUTH, MY VOICE, ALL MY ACTIONS, WHETHER THEY BE TO OTHERS OR TO MYSELF—I OWN MY FANTASIES, MY DREAMS, MY HOPES, MY FEARS—I OWN ALL MY TRIUMPHS AND SUCCESSES, ALL MY FAILURES AND MISTAKES. BE-CAUSE I OWN ALL OF ME, I CAN BECOME INTIMATELY AC-QUAINTED WITH ME—BY SO DOING I CAN LOVE ME AND BE FRIENDLY WITH ME IN ALL MY PARTS—I KNOW THERE ARE ASPECTS ABOUT MYSELF THAT PUZZLE ME, AND OTHER ASPECTS THAT I DO NOT KNOW—BUT AS LONG AS I AM FRIENDLY AND LOVING TO MYSELF, I CAN COURAGEOUSLY AND HOPEFULLY LOOK FOR SOLUTIONS TO THE PUZZLES AND FOR WAYS TO FIND OUT MORE ABOUT ME—HOWEVER I LOOK AND SOUND, WHATEVER I SAY AND DO, AND WHA-TEVER I THINK AND FEEL AT A GIVEN MOMENT IN TIME IS AUTHENTICALLY ME—IF LATER SOME PARTS OF HOW I LOOKED, SOUNDED, THOUGHT AND FELT TURN OUT TO BE

UNFITTING, I CAN DISCARD THAT WHICH IS UNFITTING, KEEP THE REST, AND INVENT SOMETHING NEW FOR THAT WHICH I DISCARDED—I CAN SEE, HEAR, FEEL, THINK, SAY, AND DO. I HAVE THE TOOLS TO SURVIVE, TO BE CLOSE TO OTHERS, TO BE PRODUCTIVE, AND TO MAKE SENSE AND ORDER OUT OF THE WORLD OF PEOPLE AND THINGS OUTSIDE OF ME—I OWN ME, AND THEREFORE I CAN ENGINEER ME. I AM ME AND . . . I AM OKAY

I can definitely handle pink shit stained toilet that doesn't flush

I don't have a problem with poopy toilet paper strewn through-
out the house

*Feces everywhere, garbage everywhere, bloody tampons on the
floor* pink fiberglass insulation hanging from the ceiling

*I've been living dirty for a long time, but the hoarding really
kicked in when I moved in with my mom thirteen years ago* two
poop stained mattresses piled on top of each other

My mom was a color-changing Starbucks cup that Hannah uses to scoop poop out of the pink shit-stained toilet

Two hoarders in black and white pioneer family portrait with two unsmiling parents and two children in stiff, old-fashioned clothes

I think it's hard because we lived together and our lives were en-twined on the side of the toilet, Sears catalogue pages mixed with poopy toilet paper

I just miss that old-fashioned lady at a writing desk painting in
a hallway of piss-filled Fiji Water bottles

She died of cancer poop-covered book about saving money

My mother's old bedroom is used specifically for Holy Bible on
a stained mattress and Aquafina bottles of bloody piss

This house has a septic issue on the bathroom door, a postcard
of Cinderella Castle, swans swimming in its moat

It's supposed to be drained once every four years pelicans landing in reeds painting on the poopy bathroom wall

When the bucket is full of pee and poop it's really hard to lift mop shoved to the side of piss-filled Fiji Water bottles

So I just put it in a smaller bucket and I take it outside and throw it out on the grass Crystal Geyser bottles filled with liquid shit dotting the front lawn

No neighbors have said anything about it to me either on the front door, a sign from the city warning the property is incurring daily fines

It's been a really long time since anybody came over dining room chairs piled with yellowed Sears catalogues opened to pictures of dining room sets with smiling families hosting smiling guests

The city has been fining me $250 a day until my yard is cleaned, and the fees are now in the thousands of shit-filled Aquafina bottles

I don't know who will help me JESUS IS LOVE on the wall in black
Sharpie surrounded by poop stains

If I was thrown out I would have no place to go Corolla with no
tires sunk into the front lawn

If you ask me how to fix the toilet—I don't know, I'm not a toilet
plunger with poop smears on the handle

I'm drinking spoiled milk, I'm eating bad salad, I'm going to eat
poopy paper filling the kitchen sink

I've been eating shit for years fecal matter in the air

Hundreds of bottles of human waste! Crystal Geyser bottles filled with liquid shit in every room of the house

All the different colors! Crystal Geyser bottles filled with shit water in shades of brown propped against the outside walls of the house

Oh no no no no no no no!

Don't leak out

RONNIE

LAS VEGAS, NEVADA

I'm Ronnie, the kid from a small town who made it big in a big WELCOME TO LAS VEGAS vintage neon sign

Walk up to my door and say open sesame! mannequins sunning on the roof of a mansion with totem poles in the yard and Egyptian hieroglyphs on the front door

I've lived on Ronnie's luck humongous lantern from the Aladdin Hotel and Casino

I was the first neurosurgeon in Nevada, and I love collecting signs, bones, satellites, canes, things made from animal parts, Robbie Knievel's motorcycle that he jumped Caesars Palace with, Venetian gondola from the 1800s, Rolls-Royces, political stuff, props that were used in different production shows on the Strip, Batmobiles, airplanes, moon landers T. rex replicas

I feel sorry for so-called normal people chair with a paper sign taped to it that says SEAT WHERE BUZZ ALDRIN SAT in blue Sharpie

They should be saving the stuff that they like Imperial Stormtrooper helmet and a Star Trek jersey

I collect medical heads and brains of people I've operated on jars of brains in yellow liquid

I have a huge collection of skulls photo of Ronnie and Bill Clinton shaking hands

I ran for lieutenant governor of Nevada in 1971 and won life-size cardboard cutout of Ronnie that says DR. RONNIE FOR GOVERNOR WHO CARES

That's what I was a genius at, selling myself Mount Rushmore replica

I built a planetarium and an observatory Challenger astronauts painted on the wall of a swimming pool, submerged in water

When I was five years old, I started collecting butterflies, and I still have that collection upstairs Liberace's glass and gold staircase winding up to the top floor where a mannequin of Liberace sits holding a disco ball

I always wanted to be the best drum made out of human skulls

I just wanted the best collection replica of "Little Boy" Atomic Bomb Aug 6, 1945 Hiroshima Japan next to a wooden sign that says ENTERING JERUSALEM, Palm Sunday, next to a cover of Hebrew Journal with DEAD in red letters over Osama bin Laden's face

When I had money, I didn't worry about what something cost
Ronald Reagan painting hanging over a herd of crumbling carousel horses

If I loved it, then I bought Liberace's piano bedazzled in tiny rhinestones with his notated America the Beautiful sheet music on it

I estimate over time I've spent about $10 million dollars on things I've collected Roman Colosseum replica

Wasn't a lot for me at the time Houdini mannequin strapped to a chair with abundant restraints, hanging upside down

I've been knighted five different times jeweled peacock

Like Frank Sinatra, I did it my way tiny Pinocchio

I even bought the house next door Hotel Continental broken neon sign, airplane with no roof, rollercoaster without a track

Started filling up the yard with old trains, railroad car seats, sign that says DR. RONNIE HONORARY CONSUL TO BELIZE, woman mannequin in a conductor's hat and shirt and no pants

Then the neighbor next to that house ended up selling their house, so now I've got three houses in a row architectural rendering of Caesars Palace in the 1970s

And, uh, it's just sort of fun light switch cover of a man with his pants around his ankles so his penis is the light switch

My wife says it's like cancer spreading from one yard to the next cross section of the human head including the musculature, skeleton, and nasal passages, Hawaiian lady lamp, headhunter statue carved in wood, real human skull, human skull carved in wood, real hog head with seashells sewn into it, poster of parasites burrowing into skin

She has total control of the corner house pelican skeleton

We don't never fight about the big house or the corner house, so I'd recommend for anyone, buy two faux Egyptian gold thrones with animal heads on the arms and animal feet on the legs

I'm $750,000 in debt; I don't have enough money to continue paying my Lifestyles of the Rich and Famous framed newspaper article on the wall, yellowed with age

If I don't pay my mortgage I could lose my replica of the Statue of Liberty

This is the tomb I'm going to be buried in—can you recognize me? replica of Ronnie lying in a iron lung inside a large yellow tomb painted with Egyptian hieroglyphs

I want to be remembered for all time peeling Jabberwocky

Then I'll go into the category of, like, Lincoln or Washington or dust in the crevices of the downed Apollo spacecraft

I'll be a piece of history ersatz Leonardo da Vinci's flying machine next to a print of the Mona Lisa next to Leonardo da Vinci's floating head

I want to be a spectacle—Muhammad Ali was a spectacle, Jesus was blue and yellow butterflies ascending in a glass wall

I want to become a collectible John Wayne mannequin with worry lines wearing a Las Vegas t-shirt

I'll be pickled, so I don't spoil Ronnie, an old man, wearing smudgy glasses and an American flag t-shirt

I made it so you can't help but remember me

GARY

FRANKLIN, INDIANA

I'm Gary, and I love plants climbing roses covering the roof, shattered skylight with a ficus growing through it, buckets of rainwater at the foot of the stairs

When I see things grow, I feel like God black mold slowly spreading across the ceiling

Because I've created vines and power cords wrapping around the banister

My house is like a greenhouse in the front hall, weeping figs with no path through, shattered pots and dank earth underfoot; every room in the house filled with plants

I started collecting plants when I was forced to retire from my job as a paramedic Gary standing in a bathtub packed with soil, clutching a dead yucca

When I got out, I missed the structure and the people in the living room, spider plants perch on chairs, leaves draping over arms; on the floor in tiny forests of philodendrons, ceramic satyrs, dancing mushrooms, laughing elves, frog drinking coffee, gnome with daisies in his beard

But some things I'd like to forget on each stair, succulents in 7-Eleven Big Gulp cups and worn men's New Balance sneakers; some cacti with arms torn, others thin and shriveled

Lifting a skinny kid in a Cinderella nightgown who drank her parents' medication they use to help with their addictions dead orchid held to a stick with gauze, reflected in a glass gazing ball from Home Depot

Touching a dead boy's brain as I put his body in a bag after he flipped his new car in the dining room, IVs drip water on raised beds filled with earth and cracked, exposed bulbs

Taking an old man who couldn't breathe to the hospital and knowing his wife would never see him again dirt on the mattress in the shape of a human

This is your job, you should be tough, you should be able to manage kitchen table filled with cooking pots of water and ivy; tiny gnats swimming in the shade of parlor palms

When my ex-wife moved my plants I got so angry Gary on a dirty mattress, a floral sheet pulled over him; over the bed, a string of lights made to look like vines; shelves of spider plants in mason jars, tendrils sweeping down, brushing his hair as he sleeps

I keep a hospital gurney Gary pushing a gurney of cacti with up-reaching arms through narrow paths between destroyed furniture and sickly yellow leaves that caress his ankles as he walks

I use it to move the plants from point A to point B gurney of cacti resting outside in the sun next to Gary on a chaise longue

I know it doesn't make sense to other people, but it makes sense to me vines twine around mildewed armchairs and end tables, grandfather clock face of the moon and stars, walls soft with rot; floors decomposing under dirt and maggots and dead leaves; on the mantel, also covered in vines and dirt, old family photos and a small garden statue of Paul Revere

GREG

WEST MELBOURNE, FLORIDA

I'm Greg, and I'm a survivor Jesus ascending on clouds ceramic figurine

Hit a tree stump in the ground wood clock in the shape of Florida

Threw me up in the air 80 to 120 feet mini trampoline

Bam, right on my head Black Cat fireworks tangled in his bed-sheets

No helmet TV on the front lawn

I was convulsing DVD inside the microwave

Blood coming out my ears rag dripping with water from the
river where he washes

Had to get flown out of there Magic the Gathering trading card

I died in the Air Jordan sneaker

They brought me back jumper cables

Was in a coma twelve days empty dresser with no drawers

It wiped out my memory bedroom window stuck open with a DVD case, wind blowing inside

My house right now looks like a cluttered-up junkyard bedroom door face down in the kitchen

You walk inside, the first thing you see is beer cans, soda cans, any cans frogs

Couches destroyed trash cans filled with water

No power, no running water kitchen sink inside the bath

Survival down here you need air conditioning chair directly in front of the stove

Water rats scurry by, I just watch photo on the fridge of young Greg holding a fish

Some of the things just don't even make sense bedroom closet with plastic hangers with nothing on them and a shelf of canned okra

I try to bring up my memory tower of boxes with an overturned stool on top

For how I was before my accident Christmas cards propped on the stool

Otherwise I forget photo of teenage Greg looking handsome

I believe I was like a ladies' man crayon drawing of clouds that says EVERY THUG NEEDS A LADY

A lot of women still talk about how fun I was wall vinyl of Patrick Star from SpongeBob surrounded by laughing seashells with eyelashes

When I came home from the hospital, instead of helping me, they laughed fabric wall hanging of Jesus carrying a cross alone

My dad and I fought water heater torn from the wall

In 2007 Dad died of Mountain Dew box ripped open violently

Checked him, no pulse, I knew it, gone Left Behind VHS set

In prayer leaning over the side of his bed wood plaque of Jesus
kneeling and praying at a rock in Gethsemane

That bring the tears out dead cricket

Can't blame no one for the clutter in my house except my stuffed
Cat in the Hat lying facedown on a clump of hangers

Have a arrangement at the gas station broken record player
with a Bud Light box on top

*I take out their trash and they let me look for cans and lotto
tickets* Christmas stocking with cobwebs

3–4 hours at a time wristwatch with an image of shepherds that doesn't tell time

A week maybe bring me 10–15 dollars Skippy peanut butter container filled with pennies

Got a winner cockroach on a crumb

.

I've thought in my mind about pulling the trigger empty gun case

Mad, sad, agitated, aggravated stuffed elephant, stuffed cheetah, stuffed polar bear, stuffed grizzly hanging by a string

Me coming back was the worst thing ever lizard crawling on a JanSport backpack

Coming back to life—most painful thing ever swarm of lotto tickets covering the floor with all the numbers scratched out

MAGGIE

OGDEN, UTAH

I'm Maggie, and I'm a single mom bloodred handprint on the outside wall of the house

On the inside of the house, we have furniture, we have clothes, we have toys, and we have demons mildewed nursery blankets her great aunt made with Raggedy Anns, one room school houses, mirror-image American flags, illegible old fashioned writing

This area is cursed line of salt at the front door

There's something here rooms on rooms filled with cardboard boxes, duct taped shut

The belief that it's cursed didn't come overnight; it took a long time to believe photo of Maggie as a teen in a Welcome to Las Vegas t-shirt

But I just saw thing after thing after thing go wrong that shouldn't swimming pool ladder leading to a brick wall

I believe the devil is after me photo of Maggie shielding her face from a camera flash

There's no way that so many different types of things and so many demons could come moving boxes filling every room in her house, filled with objects or dust

There was a suicide demon here for three days—everyone who set foot on the property during that time said they were going to kill themselves HEAL written in charcoal on the back of the house, which faces a Rite Aid pharmacy

It took writing the name JEHOVAH *on the front door and the*
back door to get rid of it on an interior plywood wall, resting on
an exposed stud, is a sign that says SET THINE HOUSE IN
ORDER in black Sharpie, with a little hand drawn house

The more darkness you allow in, the more darkness comes tiny
black hole in the kitchen floor

Demons are like the myth of vampires, they won't come in unless
you invite them box that says INVOICE ENCLOSED

Between the hoarding, which was getting worse, and me being ill, those are just open doors opening onto doors opening onto doors opening onto rooms filled with boxes, duct taped shut

When you leave doors open, things come through Maggie and her daughter watching TV on a couch surrounded by boxes on all sides

About a year ago I had a severe concussion and I was also having micro-strokes, it left me very debilitated children's playhouse wall thrown in the dirt; upside down rocking horse

So everything that I did, I did to the extreme—if I was going to
get some wood out of the dumpster, I got every piece wood and
metal siding tossed haphazardly in the backyard

If I was going to the thrift store to buy a self-help book, I bought
every one they had pile of animal bones

After I got a concussion, no one came to help, no one was there
Care Bear with a dirty pink heart nose lying in the dirt

Friend just showed up one day Maggie holding a cat skull in the palm of her hand; it has big eye sockets and sharp teeth

People have to talk to somebody Saint Joseph candle, melted all the way down

I was completely alone and had been for some time, so I started talking to Friend blanket with Bengal tigers on it blocking the window

I'd collect things for Friend—fish bones, cow bones, deer, baby rats, things I think Friend would like blanket with Tigger and Pooh Bear; inside the blanket are a wild turkey feather, stones, dirt

The hoarding got worse when I got stressed, when I was going
through a marital separation I got emotionally attached to
some stuff and I wouldn't let anybody throw away black funeral
dress

When things are good I save the vacuum cleaner dust rows of
jars and bottles with handwritten labels, all filled with dust

When things are going bad, I have this good moment set in time
that I can sprinkle around, and it shifts the energy back to good
mason jar filled with dust, labeled CHRISTMAS 2004

This dust is me cleaning up my grandma's yard after she died ranch salad-dressing bottle filled with dust, labeled GRAND-MA'S HOUSE 2008

This dust is me trying to remodel our house in 2014 when I was still trying Bragg Liquid Aminos bottle filled with dust, labeled KITCHEN CUPBOARDS 2014

If we can't get this house cleaned up and get the demons out, we're going to be homeless Maggie pouring her jars out on the front lawn, weeping

There's definitely war on earth between good and evil dust billowing up from the ground; a shadow moving in the window

ACKNOWLEDGMENTS

Hoarders is for Rollin Leonard and Lara Glenum. Thank you for your own work which inspires me so much, and for supporting me and this book through everything, including more than one force majeure.

Thank you to my friends for conversations, edits, and other support: Roland Betancourt, Pascalle Burton, Jessie Askinazi, Henry Hoke, Drew Krewer, Stephen van Dyck, Colleen Louise Barry, Mary Anne Carter, Melissa Broder, and Emmalea Russo.

I am grateful to the team at Wave, for your professionalism and dedication to poetry. Thank you to Joshua Beckman, and especially to Heidi Broadhead, whose generous and incisive edits made *Hoarders* more itself.

Thank you to the editors of journals who first published some of the poems in this project, some in earlier forms and some that did not make it into the book: *The American Poetry Review*, *Best American Experimental Writing 2018*, *Los Angeles Review of Books*, *Momma Tried*, *Nioques*, Poem-a-Day from the Academy of American Poets, *Tarpaulin Sky*, and *WIDMA: A Journal of American and Polish Verse*.